What's the "Matter"?

The Key to Creating Your Reality

Cassandra Curley

**Published in the United States by
The Messenger Book Co-op**

Book layout and cover design by Cassandra L. Curley in partnership with John F. "Cornflower" Coughenour at www.lightwerxmedia.com

ISBN: 978-1-935363-33-0

ᴈ❂ᴃ
Dedications

To three beings who helped bring me "life":

My parents, John and Carol Terry, for allowing me the
freedom to be myself
and my darling husband, Mark, for bringing light into my
life when it seemed darkest.

What's the "Matter"?

ഇൽ
Preface

This book presents universal truths by uniting innate guidance with indisputable evidence attained over the course of a lifetime; from the early questioning of doctrine as a five year old in parochial school, to listening to my father expound that "Everything is relative, Cassie"; through more than 30 years of formal education, nearly 1000 books, reams of articles, numerous workshops and over 20 years of practice as a health care professional. Most gratefully, the understanding of the nature of reality has compelled me to share.

Historically, periods of enlightenment emerge after upheaval and darkness scorn humanity's intrinsic nature of Peace. It is a cycle that recurs endlessly as our spirit concedes lovingly to our physical self.

Illumination of Life processes rests in our willingness to arouse our reposing spirit – the essence of ourselves that has been over-shadowed by misperceptions. Once more, we have reached this age of discovery as innate wisdom and scientific discoveries merge to reveal truths.

In a world often propelled by calamity and turmoil, a convergence of universal laws and science has presented an optimistic alternative to how we experience life. If we answer the question, *What's the "Matter"?*, with the response, "awareness", humanity can evolve into a revolutionary era of understanding and peace.

"I do not want the peace that passeth understanding, I want the understanding which bringeth peace" -
-Helen Keller

ෝලෝ
Table of Contents

What's the "Matter"?

ഓഃ
Introduction

"Man is what he believes" -
- Anton Checkov

There is vast evidence, supported by science, affirmed by sages and inherent in our awareness, of how we create the world. Although many contemplate this mysterious aspect of reality, even more may not consciously consider it at all. Instead, we simply know what we have been told or learned and, if we are fortunate, we have listened to our hearts. Mostly, we have simply forgatten.

Essentially, reality simply "is" — not something we often regard beyond our three-dimensional existence. We accept the physical world as primary matter. Even so, some believe Earth and its inhabitants were divinely created in seven days or, by the will of other supreme beings. Others avow the universe has evolved over billions of years. Each view bears credence.

From a different perspective, what if there were a more inclusive version - one that encompassed a unifying source? What if it were understood that all beings emerge *from* this source and play a crucial role in creating reality? Could this not prove unity of all things? Imagine a world in which science and innate wisdom demonstrated this concept as Truth while, withstanding current dogma. Would that not be revolutionary?

With this book, I present such a proposition by offering a condensed and homogenized account of how we create our physical world – individually, as sentient beings; collectively, as species; and universally, as our planet Earth and beyond.

My sincere desire, dear reader, is that by doing so, you will understand and activate the inalienable power you possess to shape your health, life and relationships with humanity.

Reality is not merely limited to what we see, hear, taste, touch or smell but is limitless in scope and in accordance with what we believe.

"Whether you think you can, or you think you can't, you are right". - Henry Ford

1

෨෬

"Reality...What a Concept!"
-Robin Williams

"Your thought is the parent which gives birth to all things" - Neale Donald Walsch, Author

In the summer of 2003, while in the final relaxation phase (shavasana) of a yoga class, I had one of several mystical experiences. Lying in what I call "nothingness", I became captivated by a bright, golden-red light that emerged in the darkness of my mind. Like the morning sun cresting on the horizon, the light intensified until a voice from within declared...

"EARTH IS UNIVERSAL CONSCIOUSNESS".

Startled by mysterious message, my first thought was ineffectually, "Whoa. That was cool!" As I opened my eyes, my mind repeated in question, "Earth is universal consciousness? What does that mean? ". This receptive state of awareness had brought insight before but, the statement left me puzzled.

After all, I knew that quantum physics has shown for over a century that **an observer instantly affects the observed**. In other words, everything is subjective, according to the observer's expectations. Existential masters and revered minds have affirmed as much for ages.

Furthermore, Carl Jung's **collective consciousness concept**, the precept that all thoughts connect to and affect one another, rang true. How else could billions of sentient beings coexist in a world that clearly responds to cause and affect?

However, "Universal Consciousness" materializing *as* "Earth"? Of course! Our planet, forever reflecting the combined expression of our beliefs, made perfect sense.

I have long known the power that mind/body/spirit plays in manifesting health. Why not expand that scope of awareness outward to include everything? If Earth is a colossal organism, replete with such bio-systems as respiratory, circulatory, skeletal, movement and metabolism, it naturally follows that there exists a planetary consciousness that interconnects them. As such, Humanity must be included.

The inspiration compelled me to further explore the nature of reality – for how can our beliefs not shape the way we see the world and what *is* reality if not what we believe it to be? The implications of such a simple premise are astounding!

I am certain that by understanding the scientific and spiritual truths of co-creation, one could discard prevailing myths that render feelings of helplessness, victimization and servitude and engage the power to create health and happiness.

2

ଓୄଔଔ
In the Beginning...

"Let There be Light" - - Genesis 1:3

Science is in accordance with the *Unified* or *Zero Point Field (ZPF)* **Theory** that states: *the universe is imbued with an omnipresent, primary field of energy that directs the creation of matter.* It has been described as a sea of light and the fundamental substance of reality. If everything that appears in the universe were reduced to its smallest component, the ZPF would be revealed as the underlying origin. It is pure energy of the lowest frequency.

Among its scientific qualities, this matrix exists at Absolute $0°$, exerts equal force in all directions and **most importantly, at every point of its existence, carries infinite potential energy – enough to materialize anything imaginable.** The crux of this entire book pivots on this principle. Therefore, I am going to restate it for emphasis:

THE FUNDAMENTAL SOURCE OF ALL PHYSICAL REALITY IS A FIELD OF INFINITE POTENTIAL.

Humanity assigns various names to this force. Some call it Universal Energy, Life Force, Vital Essence, Quantum Potential or the Field of the Absolute; in the East it is known as Reiki, Qi or Prana; the Arabic call it Qudra; and in the spiritual realm, this energy has been deified with many iconic names.

Paradoxically, to address the force with its most familiar names of **Awareness or Consciousness,** arises from itself…AS YOU.

Every Thing is energy – manifest. Awareness *is* the Zero Point Field. Of this, there is no doubt…we *are* consciousness.

Descartes, the famous 16th to 17th Century philosopher, mathematician and scientist, risked public ridicule and retribution from the church when he declared:

"I think, therefore I am".

This simple statement epitomizes the origin of physical reality. I think, therefore I must be. Our awareness creates matter. In other words:

"I Am That I Am"

-Exodus 3:14

What's the "Matter"?

3

ೲൽ
Believing is Seeing

"Our lives are defined by our convictions of who we are" - - Anthony Robbins

Intention is the mechanism that propels thought into "matter". The observer's intent belief directs the ZPF to coalesce into the appearance of "solid". We see what we believe, not the contrary. In science, this is called the *collapse of the wave potential.* **Every conceivable outcome at every point of existence remains latent until** *attention* **brings it to life! If it is intended with attention, it is so – it is a Universal Law and the foundation of Quantum Physics.**

The ZPF provides the matrix while, the material "form" arises from condensed to more complex arrangements of primal substance. We are immense fields of energy interspersed with particles **(adamantine)** that behave as adaptive units to appear "real". Paradoxically, the vastness of space between these discernable parts of form could be compared to the universe – mostly space. Like the celestial bodies in the cosmos, so are sub-atomic particles situated in the human body.

Inspired with thought and structured by intention, these units ascend from the field of infinite possibilities (ZPF) into quarks, atoms, molecules and compounds. With salient guidance, they graduate in form to living receptors, ligands, organelles, cells, tissue, organs, bones and other body parts – all of which are guided by thought and conscious of the whole.

Both inanimate and animate forms are individuations of unique patterns of energy — each fulfilling its own intention and making its indelible imprint in the world. Every part of the Universe has evolved from conscious choice:

"Consciousness gives Zero Point Field form".
     -   David Bohm, Physicist

Therefore, Evolution can be described as Nature's world consciousness fulfilling its present intention. Ecosystems, species and appendages will diminish or flourish in alliance with their collective intention. All the while, the environment adjusts accordingly.

Likewise, when *excessive* influences are produced by un-natural intention - those that are not in harmony with life - both body and Earthly systems reflect as such.

Currently, wanton industrial practices have compromised air, food, soil, and water quality, while generating rampant dis-ease. This reflection of an imbalance has reached unsustainable and critical limits. Possible restoration of balance will rely on how shared thought and intention are directed.

4

ဆဝၛ
Wholey, Wholey, Wholey...

Life is Eternal; and
Love is Immortal; and
Death is Only a Horizon; and
A Horizon is Nothing —
Save the Limit of Our Sight
  - Rossiter

If Universal Consciousness drives the creation of our Reality through Intention, profound implications arise:

✚ If all life is born of awareness, *we are one with all that is.*

✚ If we are one with all that is, *every thought affects the whole.*

✚ If the whole is affected by thought, *through volition we can change the whole.*

✚ If we desire to change reality, *we need only change our thoughts.*

And the most magnificent of all…

✚ If matter springs from our thoughts and our thoughts are all that is, *there can be no end to life!*

It is unquestionably a divine system collaborated by our collective consciousness!

The final proclamation is possibly the most difficult to grasp and the most unsettling to the foundation of many belief systems for, how can there be no end to life? The answer can be surmised by asking, "How can there be an end that which has always been and will always be?" In other words, as the First Law of Thermodynamics states: **Energy can be transferred and transformed, but it cannot be created or destroyed.**

To put this concept into biological terms: If our conception as a human began as two cells and those gametes developed from the energy that was our parents, it is even more conceivable to imagine generations as transferences of energy.

Naturally, one may say these statements are too simple to be true. Yet, enlightened beings and science have concurred throughout the ages:

"We are what we think. All that we are arises from our thoughts. With our thoughts, we make the world." - - Buddah

"The awareness of being is the door through which the manifestations of life pass into the world of form" - Gerard Neville

"Consciousness, in the state of evolution, is reality" — Itzak Benton, Inventor, Scientist

"Reality is merely an illusion — albeit a very persistent one." -Albert Einstein

5

ഇൗൽ
"The Play's the Thing"!
- William Shakespeare

"All the world's a stage and all the men and women, merely players" -William Shakespeare

Essentially, our physical self is merely a figment of our imagination – an optical illusion in this "Play of Life". Our bodies, which are implicitly driven by our intention, provide the perfect medium for this act.

Experientially, we perceive ourselves as solid, living organisms through our senses – interpreted through our sense memories and codified through feelings. However, the body is derivative. **It** only expresses what it has experienced. Ergo, the **Ego**, or the *mind's* version of the self – the persona that relies on the senses and memories for recognition, is reflected within the body. It is not our true self - for our true self is inclusive of mind, body and spirit (MBS). It is *through* **Awareness** that our totality of physical being is apparent

The corporeal form provides an ideal apparatus to stage the roles we choose. It serves as the interface, so to speak, between awareness and being – the method by which we create and process experience. How else would we be able to *experience* life if not with a body? In turn, our obedient MBS reflects the script we are currently rehearsing – acting and reacting to each drama that unfolds. As the plot changes, our perceptions and emotions modify our bodies. It takes only a change of thought to create a body of change.

6

ଞଠଔଷ
The Great Interpreter

"As a trained scientist, I'm an expert on the biochemistry of how we feel, which I believe is the demonstration of consciousness in the material world".
- Candace Pert, Phd.

The central nervous system (CNS) - the physical command center from the brain to and from all parts of the body - is the network that unites our energetic thoughts to the physical manifestation of their intentions. The following is a short version of how the biological brain achieves this:

From the ZPF (uniquely focused in our awareness) a thought overrides a calcium ion threshold in the thalamus (primitive part of the brain) to ignite an electrical impulse (turn a switch "on"). These impulses direct neurons and ligands (hormones, neurotransmitters and peptides) to convey input to trillions of receptor sites on trillions of cells (the entire body processes the thought). The information is extrapolated, processed and interpreted by the brain then, evokes an emotion based on past experience. That emotion is influenced by the current milieu and circumstances and recorded in our memory for context. Every cell in the body is aware and encodes the memory of each event but, the brain-mind remains the game master for the "physical" body.

Based on perception, how we interpret each experience translates to a belief which then affects (solidifies) the physical form. Essentially, our reality is sustained in alliance with our beliefs and our current beliefs guide our behavior. If the thought remains unchanged, so stands the belief.

Accordingly, the CNS does not distinguish between active response to impulse and simply thinking. Both thought *and* action generate electrical impulses. Your **sympathetic nervous system (SNS),** or "fight or flight response", triggers neurotransmitters, increases blood pressure, heart and respiratory rate when you *think* there may be imminent danger the same as when there *is* an active threat. For instance, you may be walking down a dark street and hear footsteps running toward you, causing a sense of alarm. If the runner passes you without incident, your body may calm down or stay alert depending on your state of mind. This primitive biological mechanism guards our survival but, is initiated by the perception. We can influence physiological processes to slow down, stop or change with thoughts alone.

A personal experience of directing "mind over matter" was while pregnant with our second child. To delay the birth a few days to bring her closer to full term, I attained a meditative state to stop four hours of labor in the thirty-seventh week of pregnancy - even though, I was already five centimeters dilated. Perrin was born, very healthy, four days later.

Our primitive (autonomic/automatic) brain system, programmed for survival, also attenuates traumatic shock by diverting fearful experiences to a storage area in the brain for safe-keeping. This allows the rest of the body to remain fully functioning. Even though we have a subconscious awareness of such events, the primitive CNS provides refuge for emotions. This protective mechanism allows for suppressed memories to be retrieved and processed years after an event for possible resolution.

Furthermore, since we are immersed within "all that is and ever was", memories are not only from localized experience but, transmit throughout existence. Memories can be universal (*collective consciousness*), genetically coded (**instinct/ancestry**), residual past-lives imprinted in our energy field, the sub-conscious (including childhood programming and suppressed emotions), as well as, consciously stored memories. Localized (bodily) memory accounts for only a minute portion of our overall awareness.

"Happiness is nothing more than good health and a bad memory".- Albert Schweitzer

7

ഇൗ
Emotion-all Senses

*"Emotion is energy in **motion**. When you move energy, you create effect. If you move enough energy, you create matter. Matter is energy conglomerated"*
- Neale Donald Walsch, Spiritual Advisor

e-mo-tion *n.* Latin: *emovere,* to move out, stir up.

If intention is the mechanism that propels thought into "matter", emotion is the power that sustains it. Together, with sensory stimulation, every thought and new event evokes a unique feeling. How we feel about an experience is captured as a perception, which then creates our perspective and becomes part of our belief system. If our perspective remains the same, beliefs become reinforced and expressed in physiological changes (DNA, chemical, structural and energetic) as well as behavioral (Ego) archetypes.

However, individual experiences of the body register only a fragment of the entire field of available information. If all sensory input to be processed by our MBS is detected through vibrations, then our five senses provide limited access. They process only partial information within the full spectrum of electromagnetic frequencies (EMF) or, vibrational energies. The full spectrum begins at 0-50 Hz, (Hertz - the measurement of frequency) in which the ZPF, brainwaves and subatomic sound fall, all the way to Cosmic Rays (10^{22}Hz). Human visible light is found in the minute range from 10^{13}-10^{14}Hz and audible sound is only detected between 20-20,000 Hz.

Further minimizing the perception of the five senses is subjectivity. Every vision, sound, scent, flavor and feel is unique to the individual. For instance, sight is accessed through the eyes *after* the brain has interpreted what it's seen (based on whatever the original identifying experience was). Like the newly hatched bird from the Dr. Seuss book, questions, *"Are You My Mother?"*, the interpretation is based on relativity. The duckling has no other basis for comparison. As such, it is understandable to see how regional, cultural and periodic styles and tastes change or remain fixed according to experience.

Equally as relevant are preconceptions of a vision before actually viewing it. The brain will hold a bias, accordingly. For example, an individual who is emaciated but, believes they are overweight, will see themselves as such in a mirror.

> *"We don't see things as they are - We see things as we are."* -- Anais Nin

Additionally, physical anomalies affect sensory perception. My husband is colorblind – making variations of colors and subtle differences in shades practically indiscernible. The seasons of the year become muted in his eyes (especially here in Florida). Despite a limited palette, the world is no less "beautiful" to him – merely different.

The remaining senses present similar physical, relative and subjective limitations; humans not detecting sounds or smells as keenly as a dog does not render those vibrations nonexistent; different music genres may "strike a familiar chord" or evoke emotions that do not resonate with those of different cultures, ages or gender; smells can trigger specific sense memories (the olfactory bulb is intimately connected to the primal area of the brain governing moods, sexual urges and emotions); tastes and touches are equally prone to degrees of limitation and partiality based on experience, interpretation and belief.

Clearly, our emotions are contingent on our ability to distinguish and discern the input of available information within any given context..

8

ଧଠ୪
Alter Ego

"*Things do not change, we change*",
- Henry David Thoreau

As stated, our physical senses present limitations to our total awareness. Like static on a radio, they also interfere with the intuitive sense. Therefore, if we limit experience to the five senses, it is easy to perceive ourselves as being simply flesh and blood (Ego). As I mentioned before, the Ego is our mind's version of the self. It can, and often does, mask the innate self.

The Ego is our imagined self. It masquerades as many roles - The Victim, The Martyr, The Entertainer, The Intellectual, The Egotist, The Beauty Queen, The Feminist and so on. We quite literally project a symbolic version, a metaphor so to speak, of our beliefs. Often, we get so immersed in our characters that it is easy to lose track of our true nature. Even our hairstyle, clothing, adornments (remember High School?) and physique can project the image we have created.

On the other hand, meditation allows the inherent voice of the spirit to be heard above the Ego. In the quiet stillness of the mind, we can hear the voice that is connected to the whole. For this reason, it is often suggested that meditation be practiced in an environment that does not stimulate the physical senses – thus, allowing easier access to a fuller awareness.

Of course, life is a human experience and it can be quite experiential to try different roles as we explore who we are. Every day we alter our Ego as we switch roles from possibly a caretaker, to employee, to executive, to student or whatever version we choose.

.

I remember myself in High School as being a student, a girlfriend, a daughter, a sister, an employee, a Class President and an athlete. In each role I projected a different image and my body stature followed suit.

The caveat of embodying our perceptions is that, in as much as we believe ourselves to be our bodies, our health is in mutual agreement. Vibrant thought induces vibrant health as dissonant thought can reflect as illness.

However, our neuronal senses do not act alone. Equally as influential at producing change are the chemical soup of emotional receptors (ligands) that simmer inside.

9

ഔൽ
Dancing to the Rhythm of Life

"Dance is the hidden language of the soul".
                        - Martha Graham

When thought triggers an emotional response - be it as mild as watching a sappy commercial or as extreme as witnessing violence - ligands play a vital role in our ability to physically experience the event. We feel the emotion with almost every cell in our body.

According to the late Candace Pert, one of the world's foremost authorities on emotional receptors, 98% of all the sensory input processed by the body is conveyed through ligands that bind to our cells – **every cell receives constant input.** These neurotransmitters spawn biochemical changes that can be felt as sensations. Many ligands are found in the digestive tract ("gut feeling") and throughout organs of the body ("feel it in your heart", "sick to your stomach"). However, none are found along the paths of motor neurons (those that send signal *away* from the brain for movement - no sensory *input*). They are unreceptive to emotion.

The manner in which ligands bind to their respective sites is through *resonance*. They vibrate at the same frequency - like two G-strings (not *those* G-strings) plucked at the same time – their vibrations naturally travel the path of least resistance (a basic law of Physics) to become *entrained* (in synch). As in a room full of stringed instruments, each with the same note plucked at the same time, they align in vibration to become entrained.

In tandem to each emotion are a corresponding combination of ligands and receptors triggered by your unique perception.

Waves of any kind that become entrained are then considered **coherent.** Like voices in a choir singing the same notes, coherence of harmonious frequencies increases the **amplitude** - creating a **stronger resonance.** Thus, the binding ligands chime at a frequency that the cells recognize and evoke a particular feeling throughout the entire body. Depending on the intensity of the emotion, the feeling can be mild or extreme and is retained in the memory of the cells for future reference.

Similar to music that moves us or people we "connect with", our emotional receptors yearn to dance in unison with like energy - they "attract" each other. They resonate.

On the other hand, when thoughts or vibrations do *not* resonate, they will repel. Do you not seem driven back by music, behaviors or belief systems that are misaligned with your own?

On the same note (pun intended), similar thoughts are drawn together to create clusters even time and space (which are human constructs) do not keep apart. Have you ever wondered why groups of people and cultures of similar minds congregate? For that "matter", if all that manifests is generated by thought, regional successes or calamities can be viewed as not only an outward manifestation of inner turmoil but, an opportunity drawn forth to demonstrate humanity's capacity for compassion.

Additionally, on a subatomic level, particles that have become entrained will, if separated, respond simultaneously to stimuli **regardless of the distance of separation!** This phenomenon is know as *entanglement* and explains the many accounts of individuals being separated and "knowing" when something significant happens to the other.

Synchronicities (another Jungian term) happen worldwide when resonant thoughts become entrained. There are no accidents – everything happens according to will.

.

10

೫೦೦೪
Food for Thought:
We Are What We Think

"No illness exists on just the physical or just the psychological or just the spiritual level. For illness to exist, it must overpower the positive forces of all three" - - Dharma Singh Khalsa, M.D.

Just as Nature seeks balance, consciousness seeks a state of accord (inner peace). When the MBS resonates in harmony with life-force, it reflects as vibrant health; when it clatters in discord, it expresses dis-ease as symptoms. Health and well-being, or the lack there of, is a reflection of processed information, manifest outwardly. Therefore, symptoms provide a metaphorical language for our MBS trinity to communicate.

Some symptoms are overt protective mechanisms, like pain as a signal to draw attention. Others may be more subtle, like lethargy or general malaise.

Similarly, but more extreme, unattended emotion or spiritual discord can be felt as a "heart attack", "cancer eating away at us" or, "unresolved pain". The body speaks to us through symptoms, in alignment with, and in order to, draw attention to our spiritual needs.

Our bodies follow inner guidance by processing information in its many forms, be it molecular, electromagnetic, intuitive/spiritual or emotional – all arising from that infinite field of possibilities (ZPF).

Molecular input includes substances that can be processed (ingested) in the form of nutrients, food and drink or, synthetic and toxic (foreign) substances. Molecular information can also be assimilated through the nose, mouth, lungs and our skin, the largest organ, through contact with external matter.

As mentioned earlier, every element in the universe has a unique structure that is recognized by its frequency pattern. Even a few molecules can be detected (this is the principle behind homeopathic remedies). Living beings identify the patterns and instinctively remember its intention (to aid and harmonize or create discord).

Electromagnetic input would include all forms of wave frequencies. It could be life-giving Sunshine, *Beautiful Music*, Healing Touch or any other frequency that transduces harmony or, it could be most forms of EMFs or similar dissonant frequencies.

The intuitive and emotional input (contextual memories) was discussed in the previous chapter.

Much emphasis is placed on what we put into or do to our bodies and whether it interferes or compliments function ("good" for you or "bad" for you). Many claims remain perennially sound but, much information changes according to current intent (pervasive beliefs, fads or marketing). There was a time when bleeding and lobotomies were standard medical treatments – not to mention all the illicit substances that were first used for medicinal purposes. What was "good" for you years ago (cigarettes, lard, "no pain, no gain") is now blamed for untold numbers of named maladies and vice versa.

Furthermore, your willingness to believe in the efficacy or harm of substances, supplements or regimens has an immense affect on their results.

Inherently, our bodies will welcome and assimilate substances that resonate and reject those that do not. Even synthetic or genetically altered versions of natural compounds do not fool Mother Nature. Animals instinctively follow this, why don't humans?

11

༉ൠ
Mind Your Own Body

*"Healing begins with the mind and
the mind is a slave to the spirit"*
- Dharma Singh Khalsa, Phd.

Countless research has shown the mind/brain is as effective in healing as allopathic (symptom dampening) methods. Partnered, it can produce a virtual pharmacy that, if unhampered, will administer just the right dose of healing or mind altering chemicals at just the right time.

"Nothing is more wondrous about the fifteen billion neurons in the human brain than their ability to convert thoughts, hopes, ideas, and attitudes into chemical substances. Everything begins, therefore, with belief."

-Norman Cousins

By simply *thinking* a substance will benefit your health (placebos are successful around 50% of the time), your mind induces healing mechanisms. My own adult children and I are testaments to this effect (greater than 50% of the time). Even though they are seldom "ill", I have never given them an over-the-counter medication (other than occasional pain relievers). My thought was to boost their immune systems and mind control by giving them a homeopathic, home remedy, massage or put them in the fresh air and sunshine, suggesting it would help them feel better — and it did. The efficacy of the treatments, along with a mother's word, saved adverse side-effects, time, money, and strengthened their body's defenses. Only one time each did we reluctantly concede to prescription medication – when my youngest had a Urinary Tract Infection and the other contracted Scarlet Fever.

I was fortunate enough to have been raised with the same sound principles and, in more than 50 years of employment, have never missed a day of work for illness.

A negative feeling toward a substance will likewise, produce unfavorable results. Input, be it thought energy, nutrients or toxins, are in synchrony with their expectations. If you think something "taboo" will do you harm, it most likely will.

Unfortunately, mainstream culture seems to thrive on fear-based ideas, as is evident in healthcare, government, many religions and family life. The "culprit" of discord is sought rather than paying mind to the source itself – dis-ease. Powerful and profitable organizations declare their "search for the cures" while seldom considering the mind and spirit in the equation. The "cause" outside ones *self* becomes the focus rather than a source of imbalance *within*. Instead of listening to the language (symptoms) of the body, we hear words like "battle", "fight" or "conquer". Silencing or cutting out the dis-ease does not address the origin.

Like the old computer term GIGO (garbage in/garbage out), the human body processes information - whether it be genetics, food, toxins, emotion, vibrations or thought. When input is corrupt, the body downloads and processes accordingly.

By realizing this, we may finally begin to exchange the "drug or surgery for every ailment" paradigm with "patient, heal thyself with consciousness".

Gratefully, there is a global growing awareness of the affect our beliefs and behaviors have had on our bodies and lives and a trend to amend some of them are proving favorable results. Food for the soul *enhances* food for the body and resists external toxicity.

"Most folks are just about as happy as they choose to be", - - Abraham Lincoln

12

ଞଓଔ
The Brain Game

"We cannot solve our problems with
the same level of thinking we used when we
created them."   - Albert Einstein

Planet Earth naturally achieves its own steady resonance, called the Shumann Resonance, and it falls around 7-8 Hz on the EMF scale (the same frequency our brain parallels when reflecting or meditating). This global entrainment is the rhythm of life in which nature orchestrates a perfect symphony if left unimpeded.

Life in its natural order is innately harmonious. Seasons and cycles, predators and prey all maintain perfect balance. It is in the Human Ego (only Humans have them), with its illusion of separateness, that disharmony resides. Thankfully, to quell the Ego and access higher levels of conscious awareness is effortless.

The Brain, *The Great Interpreter,* functions at five known levels (bands) of frequencies:

Delta – Lies between 0 and 3 Hz. These waves have the highest amplitude and the lowest awareness of the physical world. At this state, the five senses are not active and we are in tune with the highest aspects of ourselves. The right brain (the intuitive, creative side) is intimately in-synch with this state of consciousness. Neuroanatomist, Jill Bolte Taylor gives fascinating insight to this dimension in a video seen on the internet at http://www.youtube.com/watch?v=UyyjU8f zEYU.

Theta – Lies between 3 and 7.5 Hz. These waves are dominant when one is meditating or reflecting (as mentioned earlier about the Earth).

Alpha – Lies between 7.5 and 13 Hz. This is the state that most adults are in as they go about day to day tasks.

Beta – Lies between 13 and 30 Hz. This is the brain frequency we have in an agitated state.

Gamma – Lies between 30 and 40 Hz. We find ourselves in this state when we are multi-tasking and utilizing integrated processing.

As is clearly shown, the more stimulation we have, the more challenging it becomes to enter higher states of awareness. Many practices are available to help increase receptivity but, I like to follow the Outback Philosophy of "No rules, just right" – whatever resonates.

However, a simple way to detach from external stimuli is by consciously breathing and meditating (ideally amidst nature). Find a comfortable resting place with minimal (or no) distractions and begin taking full breaths (what a novel idea!). Then, allow your thoughts to gently brush away as you pointedly focus on the moment (sounds easy and it is – remember, NO EFFORT). The brain will begin to slow down and the body follows suit (entrains). You will soon be shifting out of scattered thoughts and closer to your inner voice – the place where everything connects.

To attain the highest state (lowest frequency) of consciousness is to know, completely, the unity and wisdom of all – to be aware that everything participates in Life. It does not require living in an ashram and chanting or meditating for hours every day nor, does it mean abandoning all worldly possessions and living a life of denial. It is simply retaining this awareness despite the Ego's attempt to sabotage.

Equally, with pointed attention and resolute conviction in any given action, extraordinary feats can be achieved. Professional Athletes and Olympians have stated that when they achieve seemingly supernatural strength or success they have had the sense that "time stood still".

Entrainment, the power that attracts, can be the magnet that binds us to manifest our deepest desires or, if left to the ego, can be the glue that clings to false beliefs.

13

ꙮ
"It's all Relative"

"There is neither good nor bad but, thinking makes it so." –William Shakespeare

When I was an adolescent and tried to compare my life to those around me, my dad often commented, "Everything is relative, Cassie". I am referring to the experience of being the oldest girl in a family of twelve and having very little money. I didn't think life was "difficult" but, it seemed as though most of our friends had "nicer" things and a lot "easier" lifestyle. Later in life that relativity changed when I did experience "easy". I thought, "Boy, my childhood was tough!"

As a full-time working mother of two and part-time stepmother of two, I remember feeling, "This is challenging!" until I thought of my mom, who managed it with <u>ten</u> children. She became my new gauge for "difficult".

It was not until my early forties when I witnessed probably the most challenging circumstances I can imagine a person to face. My sister's virulent husband developed the "dis-ease" know as ALS or, better known as Lou Gehrig's Disease. For over two and a half years, until he transitioned back to pure energy, I not only witnessed this strong, articulate Sportscaster deteriorate to a living corpse whose only capacity was to blink but, I watched my tenacious sister help sustain what life and dignity he had left for 24 hours a day, seven days a week. He was never put in institutional care.

In that context, I believe *my* life can never be considered "difficult". For all others, it is a "matter" of perception and each can choose whatever condition they wish to experience. My sister chose to experience her ordeal as a "privilege". Everything is relative.

Thus, we process information through our senses, decide how we feel about it and place it in a field of relativity to determine how we choose to experience it. Experience is the filter through which we base our reality.

If we allow the Ego to dominate, it judges an experience based on separateness. It judges life as "yours/mine", "good/bad", "best/worst" and so on. Unfortunately, this has been the prevailing practice in most of the world's societies throughout history. Even if practices clearly do not serve the common good, the Ego has reigned.

If instead, we set our intentions and simply observe each moment (Buddhists call this Being in the Now), without prejudice, we can decide in each instant how we choose to perceive it and our natural impulses would prevail. This is clearly seen in those few remaining cultures that have not been indoctrinated by "civilization".

Likewise, as we observe others in their behavior, we can be assured that they have derived their own beliefs in the same manner.

Therefore, casting judgment would merely be projecting our perceptions onto their realities

.

However well-intended the current polemic practices in the world's political and religious arena are, they are polarizing, rather than unifying its people. Many views have become so unyielding that they fail to even open to the *possibility* of another point of view. When reinforced, customs, cultural, political, religious and socio-economic dictums perpetuate varying beliefs. These perceptions pass on, leaving its imprint in future generations.

According to design however, life's appearance is ephemeral – moment to moment. It does not have to stay fixed. As a microcosm, DNA adapts to influences and, in the macrocosm, the earth evolves to ever-changing global persuasion. It is never too late to change our thoughts.

14

ಐಔಉ
"Brave New World" -Aldous Huxley

*"Change your thoughts
and you change your world." -*

- Norman Vincent Peale, Author of "The Power of Positive Thinking"

Occasionally, when enough of humanity determines to alter reality, worldwide paradigm changes can occur. The courage and devotion of Jeshua of Nazareth, Galileo, Leonardo Da Vinci, Abraham Lincoln, Gandhi, Martin Luther King Jr., and Mother Theresa are just a few of those who affected global change.

"Be the change you wish to see in the world" — Ghandi

The magnitude of recent worldwide events – The Great Depression, both World Wars and the Holocaust, The Tumultuous 60's and September 11 have precipitated changes that are now reverberating as two extremes – fear and righteousness or a spiritual revolution. We have decided how we feel about events and are in alliance with those who feel the same way. This is the grand design of juxtaposition working most evidently but, it need not be polarized.

Our nature is harmony but, to understand this as an experience, we have created a basis for comparison. How can we know peace, joy and love until we have *experienced* war, heartache and hatred? Now that we recognize our participation in these conditions, we can finally release fear and make the choice of our deepest desire of Peace.

ಬಂಡ

"The point in history at which we stand is full of promise and danger. The world will either move forward toward unity and widely shared prosperity - or it will move apart." - Franklin D. Roosevelt

ಬಂಡ

What's the "Matter"?

15

೫೦೮೪
Who Do You Think You Are?

"The deepest secret in life is that life is not a process of discovery, but a process of creation." - - Neale Donald Walsch

Which brings us to, "Why are we here creating?" "What is the purpose?" The answer is as simple as Hamlet's question (yes, I love Shakespeare) -

"TO BE, OR NOT TO BE..."

If we are born from the absolute (all that is and ever was), become whatever we believe (being endowed with free will), then our divine purpose is to be human – in all its many facets in order that we may experience Life.

Free will is primary. Just like love with conditions is not truly love, free will with exclusions is not free will. America's founding fathers understood this:

"We hold these truths to be self-evident, that all men are created equal, that they are endowed by their Creator with certain unalienable Rights, that among these are Life, Liberty and the Pursuit of Happiness."
-Excerpt from Preamble to the Declaration of Independence

If we heed the highest aspect of our being (beyond our senses), we *know* there is no separation and that every thought affects the whole. Therefore, every thing is part of us and we would treat all things accordingly.

In each thought we process, every word we write or speak (for words are <u>symbols</u> of thoughts) and every action we take we have the opportunity to ask, "Who do I think I am?".

During the cultural revolution of the 1960's and 70's, a book about a bird depicted this ideal.

"You have the freedom to be yourself. . .here and now". -

-Richard Bach - "Jonathon Livingston Seagull"

What's the "Matter"?

16

෪෬෪
In Conclusion...
or
"The Cave"

"There are more things in this world Horatio, than are dreamt of in your philosophies." - - William Shakespeare

Why is it that these truths are not prevalent knowledge? An answer can lie in the fact that, until the advent of mass media and the internet, information has been mostly propagated by institutions whose interests rely in the ability to sustain whatever belief system insured their survival. If we allow our consciousness to be extorted, it is easy to follow the masses and ignore our hearts.

The understanding that we are not separate from our source or each other, that we create our lives and well-being through our beliefs and that we have the free will, as humanity, to change our lives, undermines the foundation of many earthly doctrine (not to mention **MAJOR** health and political institutions).

"All great truths begin as blasphemies"
- George Bernard Shaw

At this seemingly disastrous (from the Greek, "away form the stars") time in history, it seems humanity is searching for more sensible and spiritual resolutions to the chaos.

"Out of chaos comes order", - -Unknown

For so long, many have lived an illusion, like the famous allegory from Plato's *Republic* of The Cave. In this story Plato likens "an image of our nature in its education and want

72

of education" to prisoners bound immobile for life in a cave. In this story, the only source of light is a fire which casts shadows on a wall. The captors dance puppets out of sight along a parapet above the prisoner's heads that create forms on the wall. These forms become the only reality the prisoners perceive and they grow complacent, not knowing any other existence. Until one day, a prisoner escapes to the outside to view the "real" world.

Eventually, the escapee becomes accustomed to the light and a new reality and realizes his former fellow captives are "pitiable". Plato contends that if the enlightened one were to try and convince the prisoners of what reality is truly like, they would say that his "eyes were corrupted and it would not even be worth going up".

Accepting truth on convention, hearsay or appearances alone can lead to complacency. However, if we stay tuned to our inner guidance, the truth will always reveal itself.

Countless others are broadcasting these timeless truths for the world to hear. I have seen awakened beings grow exponentially in the last forty years as we approach a critical mass of change makers. With any outcome possible in this extraordinary time, let us choose to create Peace.

ഇൗൽ

"*How wonderful it is that nobody need wait a single moment before starting to improve the world.*" –

-Anne Frank

ଐଓ
Summary

1. What we perceive as reality arises from an omnipresent field of energy, as matter, through conscious awareness.

2. Every thought is a thing that affects all of reality.

3. Intention propels matter into structure.

4. Our five physical senses mask our connection to the Universe, but allow us to experience, through the brain, our roles as humans.

5. Emotion sustains our beliefs and commands our behavior.

6. Information (in varied forms of energy) is processed, held in memory for context and affects our beliefs accordingly.

7. Like beliefs attract - unlike repel.

8. Awareness of unity is enhanced with expansive thinking (meditation).

9. All experience is reviewed in a field of relativity.

10. We can create any experience we desire through expressed belief.

ഇൻൻ
Notes

What's the "Matter"?

What's the "Matter"?

ഇൗരു
About the Author

Cassandra "Cassie" Curley, BA, LMT is a native Floridian who was born third in a family of ten children to be raised in Fruit Cove. Married for 37 years to the love of her life, they have two grown children, eight grandchildren and a successful health center in the Orlando area. She is stepmother to two from his previous marriage, step-grandmother to four.

As a business owner, athlete, artist, actress who sings and dances, Licensed Massage Therapist and perpetual student, she has been conscious of her spiritual connection from a very young age. This sojourn has brought the peace and contentment to inspire her to share insights so, others may benefit.

www.ingramcontent.com/pod-product-compliance
Lightning Source LLC
Chambersburg PA
CBHW021213020426
42331CB00003B/337